Alien<small>*nnnnn*</small>*Nation*

Joseph P. Stringer

Vivere Press

ISBN: 978-0-9903301-6-5
ebook ISBN: 978-0-9903301-7-2

Printed in Charleston, South Carolina

Vivere Press

www.chosen4life.org

All images are courtesy of Pixabay.com and
Stock.adobe.com

Dedication

For the nine saints of
Mother Emmanuel AME Church
Charleston, SC,
and for their families who taught us true
Christian witness.

and

For America, who is chosen to hear that
witness.

Acknowledgements:

I first acknowledge Jesus Christ as my Lord and Savior. Without Him, neither this book nor my life would be possible. He has given me the privilege to touch the surface of an ocean of love which is His grace.

Second, I always acknowledge my wife of 45 years, Kathleen. She is my best friend, my sharpest critic and greatest fan. Kathleen, I love you beyond words.

Third, I thank my close friend who has walked me through each thought in this book. He has been my prayer partner, friend and mentor for over thirty years. He taught me to hope when I tend towards despair. Thank you, brother Tim.

Finally, I write this book for the American people. I believe our nation was chosen by God to witness Christ to the world. Though we have run far from that calling, our people and country still shine as a beacon to the rest of the world. My abiding faith in our nation lies not in what we are today, but in what we can become if we follow God's call.

May God bless us abundantly in our calling to seek Him.

Joseph Stringer

*Aliennnnn*Nation

CONTENTS

Chosen for life, wrought in wonder, deeply loved and meant for royal splendor, you shine like the sun.

"For God so loved the world ..."
(John 3.16)

"The light shines in the darkness and the darkness has not overcome it."
(John 1.5)

"This is the message we have heard from him and proclaim to you, that God is light and in him is no darkness at all."
(1 John 1.5)

Prologue

Four sparks kindled the fire for this book.

Chapter One relates the first spark. In the fall of 2017, our church watched Bishop Robert Barron's DVD series on Catholicism. Barron's smile shows the heart of the Catholic Church today and his teaching the Truth of doctrine. I encourage you to tune into his weblog www.wordonfire.org, for straight talk on the Catholic Church and on life.

In one lesson, he related the story of a vision the Catholic monk Thomas Merton had. He saw people around him "shining like the sun."

Bishop Barron said, "We have good news to share of a love greater than we could ever know. How are we going to reach people unless we *see them as Merton saw them.* We are not called to love those who are like us but those who are different. That's what evangelism is about." Merton's image has stuck with me ever since and is the cornerstone of this book.

The second spark was the Las Vegas shooter from just before that in 2017. After an extensive search, the authorities found no motivation for his heinous act. But the story of his life painted a picture of ultimate alienation. Chapter two lays out the isolation that plagued this man. If you read through it and this book, you'll find that a part of the shooter's alienation lies dormant in each of us. We must fight his despair and isolation.

The third spark was from an Alpha course I took years ago. Thinking about sharing the good news reminded me of one of Nicky Gumbel's stories in the Alpha course. Nicky told of the time when his first child was born. He loved that baby and wanted to share that love with the whole world. He then said, "If we love Jesus Christ, why wouldn't we want to tell everyone about him?"

The Alpha course delves into the questions of life and how they relate to our belief as Christians. It's designed for those who are questioning or do not believe. I call it "Jesus 101"; if you want to get to know Him, find an Alpha course near you.

Finally, my fourth spark began almost 25 years ago. I was an unbeliever; an atheist who denied God. I was living a good life. Even though I didn't believe, I followed the commandments because they were practical. (I ignored the first four, of course.) I had a wonderful wife and family and a settled, successful career. I was happy.

Except I wasn't. Despair over the state of our country plagued me. Our alienation was the same as it is now; the same as it had been in my teens.

My problem? If Man was rational and progress inevitable, why were we still killing each other? War, murder, rape, violence, destruction and irrationality still reigned in our lives. Man was anything but the rational scientific person I had sought all my life.

We had progressed in technology but we hadn't moved beyond our base animal drives and lusts at all. How could we be "good" and still commit such horrors? I could not balance the contradiction. It drove my despair ever deeper.

Throughout the years I kept up a good mask, but my isolation grew until I found myself standing alone on a beach near Charleston, South Carolina.

I was facing a darkness I could not conquer. I had no answer. In the depth of despair, this atheist prayed to a God he didn't believe in. "God, if you're there help me. Where are we going? Where on earth are we going?" ... And God answered me. He said, "You're going the wrong way."

I had run from God for twenty seven years but when I turned, He was right there. He had really never left me. When He called me back I found the answer to my despair and isolation. The core of that answer is Jesus Christ.

I was chosen for life, to tell you that the love of Jesus saved me and transformed me. As you read through this book, you'll see a part of that story. I hope it blesses you.

For my unbelieving friends, I know the depth of what you believe, and your doubts and desires. I lived them. I want to share with you more of my journey and a greater love than I could ever offer. Come and see.

We Are Chosen for Life

What Will We Choose?

"For God sent the Son into the world, not to condemn the world, but that it might be saved through him." (John 3.17)

"There is neither Jew nor Greek, there is neither slave nor free man, there is neither male nor female; for you are all one in Christ Jesus." (Galatians, 3.28)

"Relationships are based on four principles: respect, understanding, acceptance and appreciation."
Mahatma Gandhi

"So God created man in His own image..." (Genesis 1.27)

"Where there is love there is life."
Mahatma Gandhi

One: Love

On March 18, 1958 the Catholic monk Thomas Merton stood at the corner of Fourth and Walnut streets in the center of the shopping district in Louisville, Kentucky. He was transfixed in awe and wonder. As people hustled past him, intent on errands and going about their daily lives, he had a vision. In his words:

"I was suddenly overwhelmed with the realization that I loved all those people, that they were mine and I theirs, that we could not be alien to one another even though we were total strangers. ... I have the immense joy of being man, a member of a race in which God Himself became incarnate. ... now I realize what we all are. And if only everybody could realize this! But it cannot be explained. There is no way of telling people that they are all walking around shining like the sun."[1]

---

[1] Merton, Thomas "*Conjectures of a Guilty Bystander*"

Although I agree with Merton in his last comment, I must try to do what he said is impossible.

It does seem impossible. The truth is we neither see others nor ourselves as Merton saw them. We "have eyes but do not see."

Many people will argue that Merton's vision was an illusion. People really aren't shining. We're evil and filled with hate, envy, lust, greed and more. If anything, we're like dark clouds walking around. We do appalling things. We hurt others and ourselves and create the very divisions we will discuss in this book.

Others will say that man is simply dust, a chance offshoot of natural processes. We have no meaning at all, but are a cosmic accident that will cease to exist in some future explosion of our sun ... if we don't destroy all mankind before that.

Whatever our belief, the common feeling we all seem to share is alienation.

"It doesn't matter who's in charge up in DC. Nothing really changes. We're no better off than eight years ago (or sixteen or fifty)."

"No matter what I do, I can't seem to get ahead. It's hopeless."

"Look at how terrible people are. We just find better ways to kill each other."

Read any daily headline. Watch the evening news or scan social media. We are no longer one people but are alienated and isolated from one another by belief, by technology and by choice.

Our divisions dominate us: left or right, urban or rural, Democrat or Republican, Progressive or

Conservative, white or black, rich or poor. We focus upon superficial differences, putting others into slots and categories that deny their individual worth.

Is Merton's view correct or are the views expressed in the above thoughts? In important ways, both are. Every person walking around Merton that day was, in truth, broken in some way. They were as alien to one another as we are today. There were thieves, robbers, cheats and haters. Some had destroyed their families. One man had murdered his brother. Not a single person there was pure.

That is the contradiction of man. Those who Merton saw shining were all broken. *We* are all broken. Yet I know we shine. How can that be?

We are broken because we have fallen from our original purpose. We missed the mark and did not live up to our potential. Still, the purpose, design and center of who we *are* shines within.

This is a specifically Christian vision. That we are loved extravagantly by a Creator while still being sinful is an idea unique to the Christian world view.

Let's return to Merton. Thomas Merton stood transfixed in wonder at a vision of the real essence of those people. His eyes were opened to see the deepest truth of those around him. He *loved* them. Love is the basis and the only means we have to bridge the chasm dividing us.

Love is not a feeling but an act of the will to see another, to treasure them and to honor them in their humanity. You must will to see the deeper person, to see beyond their faults and failures, to open yourself to love and to risk ... heartbreak.

Is it possible to love like that? Certainly. We do it all the time. When natural disasters hit, we join together to help strangers regardless of their belief. When evil people strike, as happened in Las Vegas in October of 2017, we shield strangers and reach out to save them.

This is the key to love and to reconciliation with others. Love is expressed in action, in doing for others and reaching out to them in their need.

We express our love of people by our actions, demonstrating a deep knowledge within us: "...we could not be alien to one another even though we were total strangers."[2]

Jesus commanded us to have an even deeper love. "Love your enemies." That type of love is such a rare sight today. Its voicing transforms us. This was the love professed by the relatives of the martyrs of Mother Emmanuel AME Church in Charleston.

Those families stood in court just thirty-six hours after their loved ones had been slaughtered in an act of pure evil and hatred. They faced the young murderer and told him, "Jesus loves you. We love you and we forgive you."

Theirs was no easy theological statement. It had to be the most heart wrenching word any of them had ever spoken. It is still the purest statement of Christ's love I have ever experienced.

Their bold declaration transformed the city of

---

[2] Merton, ibid.

Charleston. What might have been riots filled with hate, violence and destruction became a celebration of love. 30,000 people lined the Cooper River Bridge to mourn the loss and to honor the courage of those witnesses.

The solution to our divisions seems so simple. "Love one another." Yet a moment's reflection tells us how difficult, almost impossible, it is. We're not wired to act and love that way under normal circumstances in our daily lives. Without the kind of love Merton and the families of Mother Emmanuel experienced, a love born from God's view of us, we blindly revel in our own chosen isolation.

Choose now what you see. Will you focus upon the brokenness and see only division? Or will you risk seeing that each of us is "precious in His sight."

How long will we stand upon the precipice glaring down into the depths of an abyss of hate, violence, malice and destruction. If we focus only downward at the emptiness, despair shall pull us down into it.

Do not look down to focus on the darkness of alienation. Look up and across to those on the other side. They are your brothers and sisters. Look more closely at who they are — at *whose* they are. Look beneath the surface, more deeply than ever before. They *shine* with such radiance that if they were visible light you would be blinded.

"Love one another with brotherly affection; outdo one another in showing honor." (Romans 12.10)

"Loneliness and the feeling of being unwanted is the most terrible poverty." Mother Teresa

"Solitude and isolation are painful things and beyond human endurance." (Jules Verne)

"In separateness lies the world's greatest misery. In compassion lies the world's true strength." Mahatma Gandhi

Two: Alienation

No one knew him. He lived in isolation, alienated from everyone who might have cared. His father was absent most of his young life. As soon as he could, he left the family and never looked back. He had been estranged from them for years. As he walked around his current neighborhood, he acknowledged no one's greeting. Even his girlfriend, whom he had sent away, knew nothing of his inner despair. No one knew.

As he planned his attack and brought the cache of weapons up to his room, he must have thought on this. It meant nothing. The emptiness and despair had brought him to blackness. Nothing mattered. No one mattered.

He looked down on the people at the music festival, his alienation complete. He did not care about these people. They did not know him. No one knew him ... but they would.

Fifty eight people died with hundreds wounded, many for life. After months of coverage and conjecture, no one knows why and probably never will. The only clues in the picture of his life came to the surface afterwards. He was isolated, lonely, alienated. Dead to himself, he would take revenge. He would take as many as possible with him into death.

There is a stark contrast between this vision and Merton's as I related in Chapter One.

Look at the photos of the mass murderers of the past years. They stare back at us with dead eyes, revealing only a common alienation pouring from their empty faces.

We feel horror at their acts, but they are simply the extreme mirror of our alienation from one another in this country. That is our problem in America: in some ways we are not so different from these people.

We *are* alienated from one another, locking ourselves into the prison of our own prejudices, tearing apart the fabric of the nation and our sense of community. In allowing ourselves to be drawn into the division and disruption we have forgotten the closeness of family, church and neighborhood. We have forgotten how to love.

Let's note right here that the vast majority of us are fulfilled in our family and work. We are a good people who love to help and want what's best for others and for our country.

We live in mixed communities and often don't know or care what our neighbors' politics or beliefs are. We work alongside all faiths and none and accept one another without prejudice. We live happy and well adjusted lives for the most part.

However we have allowed the extreme elements to draw our focus away from solutions into a constant cycle of verbal combat which disrupts our lives and sows isolation and dissatisfaction. I write to help us focus on the good and reject the divisive.

Ours is no different from any other culture in history. Human nature tends to focus more readily on the negative — on what's missing in our lives. We easily fall into division, condemnation and hate rather than love.

I don't expect this simple book will transform us. However I write in the hope I can help us to identify our own faults and build bridges to one another.

This book will not focus on our immediate categories: Republican vs. Democrat; Liberal/ Progressive vs. Conservative, etc. These are simply the symptoms or sign posts of our alienation. To understand ourselves we must look deeper.

Many cultural and structural factors contribute to this alienation. Among those elements are the fracturing of family and close community in our country. I need not burden you with the statistics that testify to our society's breakdown. Simply look around for the evidence. The destruction of family and community has dissolved the foundations that protect us from our worst impulses.

Though a blessing, our great wealth has protected us from the consequences of our choices and shielded us from results that would destroy families in poorer cultures. For example we can afford to skate by at work, to change jobs at whim, to not work for long periods and to have government programs support our poor choices. Visit any Third World country. They have no such luxury.

In the midst of all this wealth, we are one of the least satisfied nations on earth. We have become infected with a sense of entitlement that demands more for me and wants it now!

Entitlement combined with alienation drives this wounded striking out against any opposition to our desires. The exhibitions of young college people screaming at one another is one cogent example. Demonstrations become mobs who battle one another, destroy property and murder.

In response we turn to laws and the courts. This has also become our second nature in America. We are the most litigious people in the world. We sue rather than talk. We commodify every harm, real or imagined, and seek to profit from it. Often our first response to accidental loss is to contact a lawyer to see how much money the tragedy can get us.

We are driven by politics and look to Washington for answers for every issue. We jockey, push and lobby for the power to force our ideas upon our opponents rather than reaching out to one another to change our community through our own work.

It doesn't have to be this way. By simply releasing our prejudices and reaching out in love, we can change dramatically. But we must begin by questioning our own thought processes which tend to alienate us from one another. We must critique our own ideas more fully than we do those of others. We must seek to see good in our opponents and to find common ground.

Why did I write this book now? In researching the Las Vegas shooter, I was struck by the depth of his alienation and our blindness to it. We all share in his alienation to some degree. As I stated in my November, 2017 article in the *Carolina Compass* newspaper:

"We estrange ourselves from all that is of real value. We sow the wind of isolation and are surprised when we reap the whirlwind of alienation. Weep, America, for those 58 people murdered…

…by one of us. Certainly the shooter was an anomaly, an extreme result of our society's failures. But he was also a symptom of a cancer already raging within us. If we ignore such signs, this disease of alienation will eat at us until we destroy ourselves in ever increasing acts of hatred and violence."[3]

We are confronted with two radically different visions of man. Thomas Merton's provides a view of man filled with promise and hope. The view epitomized by the Las Vegas shooter paints a picture of man as desperate, isolated, alone, lost, hate-filled and seeking death. Which path will we choose for our future? The choice belongs to each of of us. Choose, then.

---

[3] Stringer, Joseph, Alienation. "*Carolina Compass,*" November 2017

Who Are We?

Whose Are We?

"What is man that thou are mindful of him?" (Psalm 8.4)

"Does he see us here?
Are we precious in his sight?
Or are we merely dust on this tiny ball?
He hurled out into the night"[4]
Michael McDonald

"For I am persuaded that neither death, nor life, nor angels, nor principalities, nor powers, nor things present, nor things to come, nor height, nor depth, nor any other creature shall be able to separate us from the love of God, which is in Christ Jesus our Lord." (Romans 8. 38-39)

---

[4] McDonald, Michael. *"East of Eden"* 1993

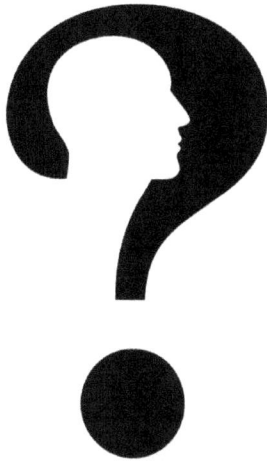

Three: What is Man

"As Diana read, she kept shaking her head. This virus, called Charon, would destroy every single human on earth. She looked up and stared out the window, thinking. *"Are there no other options? Are we that bad? Couldn't we find the way to live properly on this earth?"*

Her fingers ran along the lightning pattern etched down upon the glass. *"What did it mean, all of this? What was life for, if everything they'd done was to simply disappear in a matter of hours? If everyone, everywhere died?"* And David, the man she loved, was actively working towards that purpose.

"He doesn't care at all." A tear fell down her cheek. This time it was not a false one laced with pheromones. This time the tear was real."[5]

---

[5] Stringer, Joseph *"The Chosen"* 2015

What does it all mean? What is life for? Who are we that we could be like this?

The first and greatest difficulty in finding reconciliation between us is that we do not understand ourselves much less our opponents. We focus outward with a critical eye: we stand as judges of our past, of our culture and of other people. We do not curb our egos enough to accept that we have a great deal to learn before we make such judgments.

At the same time we fail so often to consider the most basic questions of life. "Who am I?" "Why am I here?" "Do I have purpose or is life meaningless?"

In general, we drift into reaching conclusions on these matters of the greatest import. We make no effort to truly delve into their complexities. This is another of our common characteristics.

If we hope to understand enough to build bridges to one another we must first ask the basic question, "What is man?" How we answer, either consciously or not, often defines who we become and directly impacts how we respond to others.

"What is man?" Every culture has an answer built by innumerable and unnamed beliefs, decisions, patterns and customs. Most cultures incorporate such answers in religious beliefs.

The various religions have differing views of the nature of man: from pagan beliefs that man is a pawn at the mercy of the gods; to the Eastern Religions' idea of man's participation in some form of universal consciousness; to the Christian view of man made in God's image and loved by Him.

Likewise, in the last two centuries we have added many intellectual ideologies that attempt to bring a more "scientific and rational" focus to answer this question.

Each secular philosophy sought to define or bring about the perfection of man here on this earth. Each religion seeks to guide man to moral action based on value systems (many of which are common to all.) We can see the extent of their failure in the fact that man is no different in moral character and action than eons ago.

Is Man good or an evil plague? What is the reality of Man? We must answer this question before moving forward. How do I answer it?

Man — The Contradiction

We will come to see that we have an underlying commonality in what we are. Man is *the* contradiction in our universe. First, he and every other living thing violate one of the most basic laws of nature, the Second Law of Thermodynamics, which states that systems always flow from the more complex to lesser. (For example, Carbon dating is based on this law.) But all life forms have followed a pattern of increasing complexity.

If the universe is purely material and the product of mechanical forces, then life should not exist at all. Yet life exists.

Aside from the paradox of life, what other contradictions does man have?

Man — The Irrational Animal

Is man a rational animal? He is in every area of his life except in making moral decisions. Every other life form automatically fulfills its designed purpose. The plant seeks a foothold in thin soil and bends to find the light. The lion chases down its prey. In comparison, man can survive only by using reason but violates his own purpose all the time.

Contrast our decisions regarding laws of nature, such as gravity, with those of our human nature. We follow the law of gravity strictly because the injury from jumping off a cliff is immediate. Why then don't we act rationally in following the moral laws of human nature? Because we can get away with violating them for a while. Man is a contradiction in the way he lives.

C.S. Lewis brings out this argument in *Mere Christianity*. "These, then are the two points I wanted to make. First that human beings, all over the earth, have this curious idea that they ought to behave in a certain way, and cannot really get rid of it. Secondly, that they do not in fact behave in that way. They know the Law of Nature; they break it."[6]

We fail to do what reason tells us is proper to fulfill our life's purpose. This tendency is true regardless of our beliefs and is common to us all. Our capacity for reason is like our ability to be good. We fall short in both characteristics, being neither

---

[6] Lewis, C.S. *"Mere Christianity"* Harper One Publishing.

fully good nor fully rational.

Often no one sees any result of our violations of the law of human nature. But *we* see ... deep within ourselves. The price of injustice and injury is an unavoidable guilt that haunts our nights or the end of our days.

If we constantly miss the mark, the knowledge of our wrongdoing and the resulting feeling of isolation lie heavily on us. We find every way to justify our conduct, to explain it away to ourselves. Yet guilt shadows us and adds to our isolation.

A further contradiction in our nature arises from our common understanding of right and wrong. To paraphrase Lewis, although we "know the law but break it," we demand that others obey those same laws and are wounded when they don't. We realize that such a thing as "right and wrong" exists. We are simply too quick to judge others when they injure us.

With so many contradictions, how do we see ourselves today? What image do we have of man?

The Unseen Image

Within us lies an image, a sense of life. Neither our feelings nor the self image we see in the mirror is the basis for this image. The core of the image is much deeper, built upon the sum of our cultural experience; of our beliefs, emotions and thoughts; and of our every action.

A society can build an image within us that is healthy, natural and purposeful. Or it can create ideas about who we are that are destructive to us as members of that society and that ultimately tear apart the social fabric.

Our tendency in today's society is to accept variations of an unseen image which plagues us. One form of that unseen image is the divisive condemnation of Absolutist philosophies or religions. Another form that plagued both the Las Vegas shooter and haunts our society today is the belief there is no God or higher purpose. If man is merely a freak accident of nature and the result of blind chance, then nothing has real meaning.

These are just two of the many examples we could cite which feed an unseen image that creates isolation and division. Whether held consciously or not, this image dominates our culture today. It invades our media and entertainment, our schools and universities, and our political and legal systems.

This image surrounds us and haunts every aspect of our lives. Without even our awareness it impinges itself on our minds in many forms until it becomes an unknown part of our psyche.

What are some of the forms of this image in today's dominant belief systems?

Secularism: Despairing Man, isolated from any meaning beyond the concrete.

Mysticism: Foggy Man, unable to apply reason to the beliefs he holds.

Relativism: Despotic Man, forcing others (and himself) to bow to his feelings.

Absolutism: Imprisoned Man, enslaved by

forces beyond his control and condemning any who oppose him.

Individualism: Selfish Man, regarding no others beyond his own value.

Collectivism: Worthless Man, a cog in the wheel, without value aside from the group.

The images above are the result of following the extremes of these beliefs to their logical end. Most of us have a mixture of convictions and thus have contradictory images. For instance, we're Relativists when we consider our own value systems but Absolutists when judging others. We are Individualists regarding our own rights but Collectivists in forcing our view on all others. We are functional Secularists in our modern society but practicing Mystics in that we believe just about anything today.

The contradictions have created a perfect storm of alienation within our society. If we delve into the depth of these images we discover ultimate futility and worthlessness combined with complete despair and emptiness.

This emptiness plagued the Las Vegas shooter before he broke out the hotel window and murdered 58 people. The same futility drove the murderous racist rage of the killer in Charleston. A similar despair fueled the violence between the extreme factions in Charlottesville. This image denies the existence of love and feeds alienation.

I understand the depth of despair this world view engenders. I was an atheist who denied that God exists. Yet I tried to hold onto the idea of objective reality as a basis for morality.

The belief that God does not exist impacts everything about us. Values and morals are no longer inherent in the natural world but are created by man. If man is the source of authority, the moral laws no longer relate to objective reality; they are subjective, created within our minds. If *that* is true, then nothing could have ultimate meaning; we *are* "merely dust on this tiny ball he hurled out into the night."

I lived this image. I sought out the heart of the philosophy of secularism. I found that if it were true, then nothing mattered: not my family, my wife, my children or grandchildren; not my work or purpose, nor other people. Nothing had any value.

The darkness of this total despair shook the foundations of my shallow beliefs. I looked into the abyss and discovered my own heart.

Then I knew the idea that nothing had meaning could not possibly be true. I realized *everything* has meaning. I mattered. You matter. We love and hate, fight and argue, and care deeply. If nothing had meaning we would never have known love. And I knew love. It transformed me.

Just as our unbelief impacts us, our belief in God changes everything. Strangely, faith drives us to an objective reality beyond our minds. Values and morals become based in something that supersedes me, to whose authority I owe allegiance.

In my particular case I discovered that the Creator of this universe loved *me* completely. This image filled every emptiness inside and brought me from despair and darkness into light and life. I am loved and I love. (I will tell you that He also loves you in the same way.)

The deep love of others brings meaning to life and engenders the image of value within us, which is the basis for reconciliation.

The question becomes "Who are you?" More accurately, "Whose are you?" Are you wrapped only within your own world? Or do you belong to something — or someone — greater?

What is the unseen image you hold within yourself? Had you been on that street in 1958, Thomas Merton would have seen you "shining like the sun."

Look deeply at your own core. You will find a direct correlation between loving others and discovering the true image within. When you love others you will discover an unseen image that will transform your entire life. It will change how you see yourself. It will open you to hope.

I believe the real image within you is the same Thomas Merton saw. You "shine like the sun."

"Does he see us here?
Are we precious in his sight?
Or are we merely dust on this tiny ball?
He hurled out into the night"[7]

---

[7] McDonald, Michael. ibid.

Then the Lord God said, "It is not good that man should be alone." (Genesis 2.18)

"Your work is to discover the world and then with all your heart give yourself to it." Buddha.

"[We] should seek not so much 'unity' as 'togetherness', which makes room for differences in thought and action." Mahatma Gandhi

"Character may almost be called the most effective means of persuasion." Aristotle.

Four: We Are One

The young man lay, broken. The darkness of the cave swirled and eddied around him as if it were alive. He had called out from the deep until he was hoarse. Now he was convinced he would die here, alone and forgotten. Then, from above he heard the voice. "You are not alone. We're coming for you." He began to cry.

*   *   *

"You are not alone. You are loved." Sometimes those are the hardest words to hear because we do not believe them. We feel alone, lost and isolated. The darkness swirls and eddies around us. We think the darkness is a product of those people "on the other side." They think we are the dark.

Our current culture convinces us we are alone. Isolated, lost and without each other, we have no hope. Yet we turn our backs on our brothers to build our own isolation as if it could provide us comfort. Instead of reaching out to life, we plunge toward death.

In spite of being alone and disconnected, our contemporary society thrives on being "connected." In many ways, we are more so than at any time. We see disasters strike in real time on constant social media. We respond and reach out to help those in need. "We're coming for you." That is America at our best as we respond quickly to such catastrophes.

However, in our everyday lives that same connectedness through social media makes us ignore those around us. On a recent evening at a restaurant, the room became eerily silent. As we looked around, every single person in sight was on their phone. They were texting and looking at screens rather than at the person facing them.

We were made for one another and designed to be in union together. We thirst for bonding. We hunger to belong. We seek some deeper connection that seems just out of our grasp.

"You are not alone." Michael Jackson produced a song of this title written by R. Kelly.

> "...you are not alone
> For I am here with you
> Though you're far away
> I am here to stay"[8]

Watching the video of Jackson sing this song in a huge empty venue haunted me, knowing how alone he was through most of his life. The song speaks to

---

[8] Jackson, Michael, Kelly, R.. *"HIStory"*. 1995

us. "You are not alone."

As an Evangelical Roman Catholic, I believe those words. I assure you that you are not alone. I believe in a God who loves you extravagantly. He has created us for love. Like Merton, I "have realized, you are mine and I yours."

I write this book from my Christian perspective, but read on whether or not you believe as I do. You'll discover, as we seek a deeper understanding of one another, that we share common values no matter what our belief or lack thereof. If you doubt this, read C.S. Lewis in *The Abolition of Man,*[9] where Lewis quotes the same values from every civilization and culture.

We may attempt to deny those standards but ultimately cannot. The awareness of right and wrong drives our response to others and cannot be erased. Though we reject traditional values, we create new sins to replace the "old fashioned" ones. (Is not intolerance considered the prime sin today?)

A word of warning

We cannot resolve our alienation by compromising values or by denying our beliefs. Some today call for us to "compromise" in all things, even in our convictions. We will find that an impossibility.

Finding common ground and seeing the value of one another does not mean we will all believe the same, nor does it mean we should ignore our

---

[9] Lewis, C.S. *"The Abolition of Man"* Appendix A

principles. It means we will value one another above our differences and will seek the best for others. Only when we do so can we begin to have conversations about those differing beliefs, perhaps even while respectfully disagreeing with one another.

In seeking compromise we destroy the power of morals and values. When we no longer honor each other's strength and value, legal and political means become the only way to solve our problems.

Therein is one fundamental aspect of our central problem. We seek resolution through law and politics, which by their very nature are divisive. Morality has been replaced with legal wrangling, with political power plays, and with endless national and local divisions.

If we imagine we can resolve differences by looking to our federal government, we only need look at the latest crisis. Truth is sacrificed to condemnation, division, rampant egotistical stances, vitriol and hate.

What we do not see is that the same political characters, who rant against the opposite party, sit down with them the next day. Why? Because they have work which must get done, and they work together all the time to solve problems on which they can agree.

We average citizens are the same. We work in peace together until someone brings up the latest explosive political issue. In these times, the mere mention of a name brings on the rage and division.

However we become one people when disaster

strikes. We respond to devastation like in Mexico Beach, Florida. Hurricane Michael left only slabs where homes once stood. We rush to aid people. In those times, we cease to focus upon our differences and begin to really communicate about the important realities, the first things of life.

Our eyes are opened to see the true value of those souls we help. We are the ones calling down from above, "You are not alone. You are loved."

The keys to help us to overcome our separations are the acts of serving and of helping to rebuild our community. They embody a selfless reaching out that no longer focuses upon me but upon others.

We do reach out when disaster strikes. Yet look at our nation today. Is it not in a type of permanent disaster, hopelessly divided and unable to balance the value of "the other?"

Our alienation from one another *is* our greatest crisis today. It has lead so many of us to feel like the young man in the opening of this chapter: alone and lost in unknowable darkness.

Here also is the answer to how we came to be this divided. Our focus in America has become inward and self obsessed. Our egos have driven us to rebellion against every authority.

Only in looking outward to help our fellow man can we begin to bridge the divisions we've created. Reaching out to those in need, we call out to them in the darkness, "You are not alone"[10]

---

[10] Jackson and Kelly, ibid.

"Every one then who hears these words of mine and does them will be like a wise man who built his house upon the rock;" (Matthew 7.24)

"Wisdom, compassion and courage are the three universally recognized moral qualities of men." Confucius

"Our ability to reach unity in diversity will be the beauty and test of our civilization." Mahatma Gandhi

"Our shared values define us more than our differences. And acknowledging those shared values can see us through our challenges today if we have the wisdom to trust in them again." John McCain

Five: We Are Together

I went white water rafting a few years ago on a river near Pittsburgh. It was great fun; challenging and scary. The guides were very specific in teaching us, "If you get thrown from the raft, keep your feet up! If your feet get caught under a rock, the current will lay you down and you will drown. We won't find you for months if at all."

I was thrown from the raft. We passed over a hydraulic that built pressure underneath until the raft flipped. One instant I was paddling like crazy and the next instant thrown underneath. When I came up the guide was there screaming at me, "Feet up! Feet up!" I had fun. I left alive but with bruised ribs.

I guess the attraction of white water is the balance between the beauty and freshness of the river, and the danger and death lurking beneath. Some people love it. Once was enough for me.

*   *   *

Our lives are all lived within what we might call the river of life. Sometimes the current is smooth and guides us along and sometimes turbulent, tossing us about the boat. In this way the shape of the culture also contributes to the stability of the boat.

Our own culture is much like an extreme white water experience. We're in our particular boat paddling like mad. Currents enter the river from every direction and are too swift and strong for us to hope to fight them or resist. We are on a headlong plunge deep into a canyon of hate and destruction. The rocks are everywhere above and below the water line. A sudden change of pressure can throw us from the boat and quickly harm or even destroy us. There seems to be no way out and no respite.

We are together in this boat with no other way to navigate the river. To swim it alone is death. Even to attempt to paddle it alone is impossible. We must paddle together to navigate the currents. If we work at cross purposes we will all drown. Yet we are all busy paddling in different directions.

What do we have in common? We all believe that Truth and Falsehood, Right and Wrong, and Good and Evil exist. We differ radically on how we define what is true or false, right or wrong, good or evil. But the idea of those concepts is universal.

The reality of our human nature weighs heavily upon us. We rebel against our nature in so many ways but in doing so distract ourselves from the pure core of our design. That very rebellion fuels our isolation.

A part of us wants to be alone. As individuals and as groups we create division to insure our alienation rather than build bridges to discover our common human nature.

Part of that division is our natural quest to find our roots. We are of this family; of this faith or belief; of this nation, not that. Often we seek justification for the many actions we regret, or find a belief system or practice that supports our world view and helps us define our lives in our own terms.

Faith traditions used to be the sole focus of those world views. During the last two hundred years other philosophies have been developed that attempt to explain the world apart from faith. Our connection is that we all are driven to find ways to understand our place in life.

What else do we have in common? We believe human beings have some kind of "rights" which privilege us to be treated in certain ways. We all feel some responsibility toward others. We have an inbuilt longing to see our circumstances get better.

More essentially, we are searching for something missing we yearn to find. That yearning is much deeper than simply a taste or desire. It resonates within our very bones. We thirst and hunger for love. We want to love and to be loved. All of us also know these common things.

Commonalities

As we delve into our nature, we find other contradictory commonalities of Man:

He dreams of a better world and despoils this one.

He seeks justice and excuses his own actions.

He acts with self interest and in self-defeating ways.

He is kind and cruel.

He is passionate and apathetic.

He is focused and distracted.

He is giving and selfish.

He pledges on his honor and cheats.

He gives life and destroys it.

He desires good and does evil.

He is as glorious as the angels and as horrible as the devils.

The remarkable thing about this list is that it could describe a single man or woman. And, the list could go on much longer. Our similarities far exceed our differences.

These are just some of the commonalities that hold us together. Why then do we seek so often to divide and separate ourselves? I might say this tendency is also common to us all. We need strong community to survive, yet our nation seeks to abandon everything holding the boat together.

What are the elements of strong communities? The positive aspects of our character build us up. Those aspects are learned and practiced first in family and then in church, synagogue, mosque or school. With just a bit of self observation, we know we don't automatically do those on our own. We must learn respect, kindness, compassion, focus, forgiveness, goodness and more.

Many Americans admire the resilience of

nations like Britain, France or Italy who sustained terrible losses in the wars of the twentieth century. We admire the steadfastness of our grandparents who lived through the Great Depression and then war. One of the basic elements of their resilience is the close family and community ties that carried them through the worst man can do.

Their boats survived the raging rivers of war and devastation because they rowed together to overcome those disasters. We have done the same in times of crisis but now, instead of finding ways to work together, we seem intent on tearing apart the fabric of the raft that holds and saves us.

The contradictions which drive this destruction of our social fabric are: Rebellion, Condemnation, Distraction and Apathy. These four tendencies which we all have alienate us from one another and convince us that we must paddle on our own; that we have no other choice. They are the foundational reasons that we can't talk.

In the following chapters we will review each of these elements of alienation which are common to us all. There *are* healthy alternatives, but to varying degrees we have chosen the negative and isolating option rather than healthy one which counterbalances it. This is why we can't talk.

Why We Can't Talk

"Now the serpent was more subtle than any wild creature that the Lord God had made. He said to the woman, 'Did God really say ...?'" *(Genesis 3.1)*

"But the Centurion answered him, 'Lord, I am not worthy to have you come under my roof, but only say the word and my servant shall be healed. For I am a man under authority ...'" *(Matthew 8.8,9)*

"Without feelings of respect, what is there to distinguish men from beasts?" *Confucius*

"To lose patience is to lose the battle." *Mahatma Gandhi*

Six: Rebellion or Respect

"'Question authority.' That's what I always endeavored to drill into my students. 'Question authority.'" My science teacher friend and I were arguing over a political issue.

"'Question authority?' That's what you teach? You a science teacher and a Catholic? 'Question authority.' Isn't that exactly what the serpent said to Eve in so many words? 'Did God really say ...' He made her question authority."

My friend just shrugged. He could not understand that the way he was teaching is one of the foundations for our problem in the world.

Question to learn

Is there a right form of questioning? In arguing with him, I did not mean we should not question at all. It's obvious that we learn by questioning.

The problem with the focus of my friend's teaching was that it did not encourage his students to "question authority" with knowledge. It reinforced his student's ego by placing their shallow understanding on a par with their teacher's. Too often, young people are encouraged to rebel against authority without the background needed to do so wisely. This was *my* earliest error, born of my ego. Ego rebels against any authority over it.

Question to rebel

Our culture *is* in rebellion. We do not want to listen to logic or reason, especially when the ideas contradict our accepted "knowledge." We will not listen to arguments that make sense if hearing the truth requires us to change our ways.

Rebellion is the core of alienation. In this age, we reject our parents' wisdom. We challenge the lessons of history as irrelevant. We ignore the lessons of the church (or of any other authority who could teach us value outside ourselves.)

Many people now rebel against nature itself. They no longer recognize man has a fixed nature, much less that there is an existence outside the control of our own minds.

The Dictatorship of Feelings

This rebellion against nature has been taught for generations. We accept *this particular* authority because it allows us to pursue our feelings. If reality and reason do not exist, I can do as I feel like and others have no basis to question me. However, we know our feelings are notoriously unreliable.

What happens when the other person requires me to accede to his feelings? Without a separate objective reality, we cannot decide either who is right or if right and wrong even exist.

Question Authority

Our modern ego is the source of our rebellion. We are the most egotistical people in the history of humanity. Ego fuels rebellion because we value our independent minds above all authority.

We look down upon all past civilizations and our contemporaries in the Third World as lesser beings and scoff at their lack of empirical knowledge. Yet our memories are short. Look up a 1912 eighth grade exam. Could you pass? The classics, ethics or logic are no longer studied in school. Our grandfathers could read Latin and Greek ... and it was not an unusual talent. Our knowledge has become much more extensive but more shallow.

Our civilization is certainly more advanced in technical wizardry and scientific knowledge. Those tools have given us the ability to transform our physical world, creating great advances. We have conquered many diseases, lifted much of the world from abject poverty, and become masters over much of nature. These gifts merit great celebration and hope. We *are* physically much better off than even a century ago.

However, have our moral lives changed at all? Are we better people than our grandfathers, or the Romans of 2,000 years ago, or the Greeks or Egyptians who lived 4,000 years ago? With a minimal study of history, we will be humbled. *Nothing in our character has changed at all.*

Name any evil. You will find it present in all cultures and every civilization throughout history. We know as little about our inner drives today as ten thousand years ago. If we believe in man's moral progress, we truly must have blind faith.

I understand rebellion. When I decided I no longer believed in God, I had to *not believe* on blind faith. I was a product of the 60's: *"God is dead. Free love. Science has the answers. Reason will reign supreme. Faith is myth. Man will progress and free himself from the tyranny of the past."*

I thought of myself as independent but was just a follower, seduced by the spirit of the times. I decided I had to choose between "faith and reason" and "science and religion."

To believe the arguments of my friends, I had to put on blinders. I did not want to question too deeply. I would not research arguments. I did not read C.S. Lewis, or G.K. Chesterton, or Thomas Aquinas or Augustine. I would not listen to Billy Graham or Bishop Fulton Sheen, much less read the Bible.

Why did I rebel with so little foundation to do so? I wanted to rule my own life. If I researched the arguments for God, I might find real arguments for faith. If God exists, then I could not do certain things

I desired. But freedom from authority did not set me free. It enslaved me to my own desires which eventually began to be destructive.

Respect

In contrast, having been called back to God I now describe myself as a man under authority. "The first lesson we learn from God's law is that *the Sacred exists*..and it is *not me*. God is God. I am not."

"Wow! I am *not* the master of my fate. I am *not* the captain of my soul. What a relief! If a Sacred God exists, there are standards apart from my own. I answer to Him. (Thank God)."[11]

Even after my return to faith, one of the most difficult tasks for me was to put myself under authority. My statement above freed me to question, to doubt, to argue and finally to believe.

Inescapable Authority

The paradox is we cannot escape authority even while denying its power. No one ever says, "I just don't believe that because I feel it." People argue they are right, but they always justify themselves as to why they are right and you are wrong.

Authority is just an extension of that argument. We attempt to justify our point of view by pointing to various experts. There are plenty around these days to

---

[11] Stringer, Joseph "*The Ten Commandments for Business*" 2015

prop us up and smoothly tell us, "You're right, right, right. Go that way. It's easier! Don't question yourself. Ignore contradictions. You know better."

Those are false teachers who have either their own purpose in furthering our destruction and solidifying their power, or have been taught error themselves by a culture fraught with rebellion.

There are ponderous authorities on each side. Obviously, I am citing my own in this book to illuminate my point so *please* examine mine.

What are we to do since we live in a society more varied than any in history? Our nation is a melting pot of different cultures all drawn here in the hope for freedom. This nation has every religion and the growth of the "nones" who say they have no belief. Even science is in dispute. (Global warming or genetic engineering are examples.)

Respect and Argument

G.K. Chesterton commented some 85 years ago, "Unfortunately, there are many who do not understand the nature of any sort of argument. Indeed, I think there are fewer people now alive who understand argument than there were twenty or thirty years ago ..."[12]   It seems we have continued to lose the ability to rightly "argue"; to dispute with reason.

The first thing we must do is rediscover "argument." Today "argument" means hurling

---

[12] ChestertonG.K. "St. Thomas Aquinas, The Dumb Ox"

invective at each other. We have forgotten the craft of using logic to reach the correct conclusion in any disagreement.

One of the most divisive and common errors in our culture today is that one can't argue about morals or beliefs; that those are only feelings, opinions or tastes; and they are not subject to reason. If this were true, on what basis could we even agree on anything? We would be unable to create any standards as a basis for a culture or civilization.

Every single society has moral codes fully established through customs that eventually become solidified into what we call law.

The difficulty is they can't all be right. Each religion or ideology has elements of truth which require reason to discern the good ideas from the wrong ones.

So we must relearn *how* to argue. The first element of practical argument is *respect for the other.* In arguing, one must not attack the person himself or his motive. We can only properly listen if we *see* the other person as a human being, worthy of our time, who has possibly made an error in his thinking.

Listening with Respect

Errors in thinking are like an illness. Just as a doctor seeks to correct a physical illness, we want to find the cause of our opponent's "thinking illness." Just as the doctor listens to our breathing and heartbeat, we must *listen.* To listen to your opponent's argument, *first hear his heart*. What underlies his ideas? Don't think of how to answer. Hear who he is as much as what he is saying.

"Our Community Listens"[13] is a worldwide movement begun in 2008. Its three day courses teach people attentive listening skills. The core of their course teaches respect for the other person in our listening habits. People who have taken the course say their lives have been transformed simply by learning how to properly listen to others.

So our answer in argument is to honor the person and to respect him before we begin to critique his argument. His worth is deeper than the argument just as our health is deeper and greater than the illness plaguing us.

Respect and Patience

Gandhi said, "To lose patience is to lose the battle." We *are* impatient and want easy answers *now*. We become belligerent when our needs are not met.

We are entitled! "How dare you keep me waiting. How dare you not solve the current crisis right now and expend all your energies on me."

This is Ego speaking. "I have my own belief and give you no time or thought for yours. I am the focus of my life." But is this the way to understand others? We will never be able to do so unless we respect one another. We will not respect unless we

---

[13] www.ourcommunitylistens.org

find the patience to really listen.

But we cannot listen when locked into the fortress of ego. We rail against the "enemy," who is anyone who dares oppose us. We rebel against the love of others.

"Love one another." We place so many obstacles in the way of that simple rule, searching for ways to deny love. We use others for our own ends. We shove them aside in our impatience, refuse to listen to them, deny their worth and will not recognize they may have answers we need.

But our heart's cry will not cease. Our minds will not be still. The underlying emptiness of the *things* we grasp at can never fill the essential need for each other.

Our need for one another is like the air we breathe. We thirst for love. Love stands right before us. Look up and out!

Alone we hide in the shadows
But together we bring on the light
One voice is not strong enough
One heart just won't do
In this world I don't count for much
Unless I stand for you[14]

What other essential character flaws of man contribute to our alienation and prevent us from loving one another?

---

14 McDonald, Michael *"Blink of an Eye"* 1993

"Do not judge, and you will not be judged. Do not condemn, and you will not be condemned. Forgive, and you will be forgiven. Give, and it will be given to you. A good measure, pressed down, shaken together and running over, will be poured into your lap. For the measure you give will be measure you get back." (Luke 6.37-38)

"The weak can never forgive. Forgiveness is the attribute of the strong." **Mahatma Gandhi**

"Those who cannot forgive others break the bridge over which they must pass." **Confucius**

Seven: Condemnation or Forgiveness

"But Jesus bent down and started to write on the ground with his finger. When [the Pharisees] kept on questioning him, he straightened up and said to them, "Let any one of you who is without sin be the first to cast a stone at her." Again he stooped down and wrote on the ground.

At this, those who heard began to go away one at a time, the older ones first, then the younger, until only Jesus was left with the woman still standing there. Jesus straightened up and asked her, "Woman, where are they? Has no one condemned you?"

"No one, sir," she said.

"Then neither do I condemn you," Jesus declared. "Go now and leave your life of sin." (John 8.6-11)

*   *   *

If you've read through the gospels, you know

Jesus spent a lot of time with those who were the outcasts and sinners of his day. They included people who had truly done wrong. How did he treat them? In each case, he did not condemn them. He first got to know them by engaging with them in conversation. In the midst of questioning them he would speak the truth to them about their actions.

In the example of the woman caught in adultery, Jesus refuses to join in the condemnation of the woman but instead points indirectly to the sin of the accusers. After they all leave he too refuses to condemn the woman but sends her away, telling her to sin no more.

In every engagement with sinners Jesus does not shy away from speaking the truth about the wrong that people have done, but he does so in a way that does not condemn but draws them to see their own error and correct their ways.

"Who are you to judge?"

We have to be very careful here. Too often we use the injunction "Judge not" as an excuse to cover what we know is wrong. "Who are you to judge?" Yet we all judge and must judge or we could not even live together.

Jason Staples speaks of this in his blog "Misinterpreted Bible Passages." "Judgment involves making the distinction between good, bad or indifferent, not simply declaring something to be bad. We cannot possibly go through life without judging; every decision we make implies a particular value judgment underlying it."[15]

One of the primary points he makes is, we all judge and must do so. We have a universal understanding that "right and wrong" exist. We may have differing understandings of the right but to even determine something is "right" we have judged. We can't get away from it.

Condemnation

Yet too often we turn that judgment of right and wrong into condemnation of the person we think is wrong. We must take great care not to do so.

We are all too quick to judge and condemn others no matter our belief. Both sides of any dispute jump immediately to character assassination. They do not seek to know one another. *That* would be too dangerous. They might find things in common.

We Christians have been specifically warned about judging others, but we have forgotten the meaning of Christ's words. Instead of reaching out to others we stand like the Pharisees did, judging those around us. We too have joined in the chorus of hate in condemning others rather than approaching them.

The great problem with judgment is it prevents us from engaging those we think are wrong. They will never listen. And when we condemn, *we are not listening either.* We stare upon the sin we see

---

[15] Staples, Jason *"Misinterpreted Bible Passages"* 9/1/2009

and refuse to discover the treasure within.

This does not mean sin and wrong do not exist or are subjective, changing with the viewpoint of the person. They are real, objective and viciously destructive to our lives. We do not ignore the sin or excuse it. But we are called to delve deeper into the person we engage.

Stephen Altrogge points out a middle ground between condemnation and open acceptance of wrongs. "When I see someone sinning, I can acknowledge that it's sin in need of repentance, but I can also say, 'Tell me more.'... Compassionate judgment seeks to stay faithful to Scripture while also truly loving the person who struggles."[16]

Forgiveness

Acceptance of all wrong is certainly not the answer to condemnation. What is? Forgiveness. Read the opening Bible passage of this chapter. We so often cite the beginning admonitions regarding judgment, but we ignore the following promises. "Forgive, and you will be forgiven. Give, and it will be given to you. A good measure, pressed down, shaken together and running over will be poured into your lap."

"Do not." The negative precept leaves us nowhere to go. The positive opens out for us such promise of fulfillment. "Forgive ..." "Give ..."

What do we think Jesus means when he says,

---

[16] Altrogge, Stephen *"The Blazing Center"* Nov. 27,2017

"... it will be given to you. A good measure, pressed down, shaken together and running over ..."

What a promise of extravagant and overflowing blessing. Where might it come from? Perhaps from the blessings poured out to us through the love and friendship gained by giving of ourselves to those we would have condemned.

We might discover hidden secrets within their hearts. We may learn their heartache and weep with them. We could feel the compassion for them which brings them to life and makes them "shine like the sun." We will discover that we love them.

Again, this does not mean we excuse or ignore the wrong they do. (Or we might discover the wrong was truly our own.) We love them as God has loved us, even while we were still in sin. "God showed his love for us in that while we were still sinners, Christ died for us." (Romans 5.8)

Do you see how condemnation closes off any possible means to reconcile with our opponent? Only in forgiveness for the hurt they may have caused us or others, and in giving of ourselves to reach them can we discover the treasure of who they are — and rediscover who we are.

I can tell you of the transforming power of forgiveness. It will pour out blessings upon you. Thus it was for those of us who witnessed the forgiveness given by the relatives of the Mother Emmanuel Nine. It changed everything in Charleston. It transformed us and gave us transcendent hope.

"Set your minds on things that are above, not on things that are on earth." (Colossians 3.2)

"...You will find that anything or nothing is sufficient to attract his wandering attention. You no longer need a good book, which he really likes, to keep him from his prayers or his work or his sleep; a column of advertisements in yesterday's paper will do. ...You can make him do nothing at all for long periods."

"...'Nothing' is very strong: strong enough to steal away a man's best years, not in sweet sins but in a dreary flickering of the mind over it knows not what and knows not why." (The demon Screwtape's advice to a novice demon, Wormwood.)[17]

---

[17] Lewis, C.S. *"The Screwtape Letters"*

Eight: Distraction or Focus

Recently my wife and I were eating diner in a small restaurant. While we spoke we suddenly realized the restaurant was eerily quiet. We looked around. Every single person in the restaurant was on their cell phone: old and young adults, teens, children. *Everyone.*

I don't need to cite you statistics on our addiction to technology. Just look around. We have become prisoners to those tiny screen gods. We serve them, doing digital prayer, our hands held together, cradling the god between.

We scoff at stories of the ancients who fashioned images of gods from hammered gold. They bowed down to worship those false images. Are we so different, enslaved to our small screen gods? We live our lives with heads bowed over the screen, looking down. We fail to see those we love who sit right before us.

Distractions

We have a thousand Facebook friends we've never met face to face, with whom we've never shared a meal. Meanwhile we ignore our real close friends or family for days or months or years.

We haven't sat down to a family meal in ... I can't remember. We don't play board games together, or lawn games or a pickup game of catch. Our kids don't play hide and seek or tag. They're too busy going to soccer or T-ball or gymnastics or dance or music or ...

We don't sing together around the piano. (Imagine it. Our parents or grandparents used to do that!) We listen to our own music on headphones, locked in isolation from anyone else in the room.

We never speak to anyone on a bus or in the store or even in church. We rush in, get our task done, and rush onto the next activity.

We are the most connected civilization in history — and the loneliest. Suicide, mental illness and other symptoms of our endemic isolation are growing in geometric proportions.

We are the wealthiest nation in history — and the least satisfied with what we have.

We have the greatest capacity to enjoy a life of leisure — and live the most frenetically paced lives on earth.

Do we see a pattern here? Are we happy? It

certainly doesn't seem so with the constant barrage of hatred and division in the news, on the email feed, on social media and among those we know. Are we really connected or have we substituted the reality of our relationships with the "nothing" of distraction.

When we are not distracted by our frenetic activities, our work dominates the rest of our time. The structures of modern work contribute to our alienation, placing us in cubicles that separate us. The newest work positions are IT, programming, data mining and research. These all require focus on our monitors and often can be done at home or anywhere. We have less and less connection at the office.

In addition to the way our work is structured, an incredibly fast-paced atmosphere of constant distractions interrupts our work: phone calls, emails, texts, chats, video conferences.

Add to those the personal calls and texts we get and the time we spend with distracted surfing on our work computers. We read news feeds, buy things we really don't need, surf porn sites — and suddenly hours have passed. Temptation comes to us at the speed of light. It's amazing we find time to actually work, much less make friendships in the office.

Is there any relief from this constant barrage of distraction? A day off? We used to honor a day of rest, the sabbath. So few companies today recognize our need for rest. Those that do, like Chick-fil-A, present a beacon of peace and hope amidst the raging current of our distractions.

Lewis' demon Screwtape, who I mention in the

opening of the chapter, has been working overtime on us. We find every way we can to do "nothing" and fritter our lives away. Distraction is a pandemic stealing the minds and hearts of everyone.

One terrible symptom of our distraction is we are losing our ability to concentrate. The pulsing images on our video games are rewiring our brains to respond to quicker, changing patterns and rapid responses that provide immediate gratification.

The result is we are unable to retain our focus long enough to carry logic through a sequence to its conclusion. Is it surprising then that we cannot properly "argue" as I described in chapter six? We literally are losing the capacity to think deeply. Thus, we stoop to attacking the person rather than dealing with the argument.

What is our answer to this problem? How can we fortify ourselves against distraction?

Focus

One way has become popular among many: meditation. The Eastern religions have given us a great gift in their focus on training the mind to rid itself of outside distractions. There are also traditions of meditation in other religions, including Christianity.

We must find the time for undistracted quiet when we can concentrate on those closest to us, on family and community. When did we last take the time to find a quiet place and drink in the beauty of our spouse or our children or an early sunrise?

We have forgotten the value of silence, of quiet contemplation. Our lives are too full of noise. How can we hear over the din of our modern lives? How see clearly beyond the distractions and sin that bombard us at the speed of light?

"They have ears but do not hear. They have eyes but do not see." If we disconnect from our constant distractions, our sight and hearing will return and we may once again find our proper focus.

How will a better focus help to heal our divisions? If we can set aside the distractions that plague us we will gain valuable time for living with *purpose.* We can have the time to reach out to others and get to know them.

However, will we actually take the time we need to do so? Do we care enough to reach out? Or will we continue in our comfortable lives filled with the distraction of nothingness? Can we break out of our apathy to reach across the divide?

Our next challenge speaks to this issue.

"I know your deeds, that you are neither cold nor hot. I wish you were either one or the other! So, because you are lukewarm — neither hot nor cold — I am about to spew you out of my mouth. You say, 'I am rich; I have acquired wealth and do not need a thing.' But you do not realize that you are wretched, pitiful, poor, blind and naked." (Revelation 3:14-17)

"No man loses his freedom except through his own weakness." Mahatma Gandhi

"Truly, I say to you, unless you turn and become like children, you will never enter the kingdom of heaven." (Matthew 18.2)

"And do not be conformed to this world, but be transformed by the renewing of your mind, so that you may prove what the will of God is, that which is good and acceptable and perfect." (Romans 12.2)

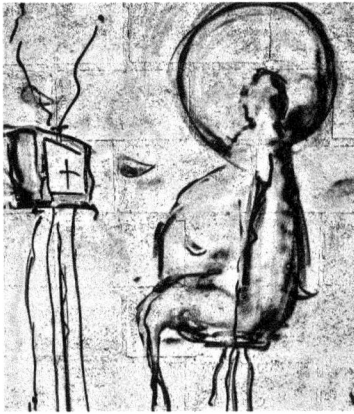

Nine: Apathy or Passion

They began to make their way south through empty fields. Skeletons lay unburied all around, the bones bleached from the weather. They were the only evidence of human life, the vestige of total war in America. It was evident these people had died in vicious hand to hand combat with primitive weapons. Their bodies had been stripped and left to rot.

Grace was visibly upset. She had not directly seen the effects of this terrible war. "Roger, how can this be? How could they leave them to an unholy end like this? Didn't people care?" She gripped his hand in anguish.

Roger had lived through much worse in this war. "No. They didn't." He fell silent.

They walked on for several more miles. Roger finally spoke. "These people were murdered for hate or greed or sheer animal survival. Some for no reason at all. They didn't care enough to bury even those they loved. There were too many. Millions…"

His voice faded off into a strained silence again. He kept shaking his head, trying to relieve the pressure of this knowledge. "Perhaps it's better they didn't live. Maybe we should all be left to rot without burial. How do we care so little? I don't know!" He dropped Grace's hand and stalked off.[18]

Apathy

"How do we care so little? Will we stand aside and watch the extreme forces on both sides destroy our nation? Do we care enough to reach across the divide? If we do not stand against this alienation from one another, I see only a great devastation in our future. War and endless destruction.

Our greatest challenge is not rebellion or condemnation or distraction. It's that we don't care enough to break our chains though they hardly bind us. Our problem is one I wrote about years ago: the shallow grave of Apathy.

The vast majority of Americans stand in the center between the extremes. We simply want to live our lives, enjoy our families and communities, and help find solutions to our nation's problems.

Yet we find our emotions hijacked by an extremely small percentage of radicals whose actions sow our divisions and tear the nation apart. I see articles in blogs on both sides questioning, even hoping that we are headed towards civil war.

---

[18] Stringer, Joseph *"The Chosen"* 2015

What do those radicals have that we lack? Zeal. They are filled with fire to achieve their goal. They are focused with obsession upon a goal of rebellion against what they see as injustice. They condemn our apathy ... and rightly so.

America is not immune to this type of surrender to radicals, nor are we alone. Less than ten percent of Germans were Nazis, yet the National Socialist party took over the country, began by killing their own and almost destroyed Europe.

The same is true of many other dictatorial nations or systems today. The people are too afraid to stand for their own freedom and throw off the yoke of those who comprise a tiny minority of the population. Apathy and perhaps a very real fear paralyzes them.

Where will we find the passion to bring us to reconciliation? Usually one man stands and will not bend. The young Chinese man stood against a tank in Tiananmen Square in Beijing. Vlacav Havel lead the nation of Czechoslovakia to freedom. Gandhi sat down against British tyranny. Here in America, Martin Luther King withstood water cannons, beatings and jail, and was finally assassinated.

Where is the leader who will stand for us today and say, "No more. We will not give in to the alienation which seeks to tear us apart. We will find peace and forgiveness and work together once again."

Perhaps he does not exist and it will be up to us together to take back our nation and right its course. Is our nation mired in this rut of apathy simply because no one has appeared to lead us?

The more likely explanation is we just do not care. We have forgotten who we are. We are focused on political solutions, which means asking others to do the work to resolve our problems. When will we take responsibility for our lives and for our actions instead of demanding that the federal or state government or anyone else do so?

A great pandemic is sweeping the civilized world. This disease infects vast numbers of people, from the smallest village wrapped in comfort to the largest city filled with indifference to the greatest nation on earth now conquered by mediocrity. The disease is apathy, a luxury born of the wealth of a society so advanced that we can afford to simply not care.

So many people lead empty lives devoid of purpose and lacking real depth. They drift along at home and work, hoping just to get by. Their work is characterized by TGIF that starts work Monday waiting for Friday to get here.

What we feel in America today is not the great striding forward of moral giants but the grey numbing fog of a society in drift. Our moral compass is lost. What is our national goal outside fighting the latest political pseudo-crisis?

Personally we drift along through lives that feel like ruts, being run in circles by our culture and not in control. Busy, frustrated and unfulfilled, we cry out in despair for something more, for some deeper meaning. All of this apathy ends in alienation from one another. We don't care enough to reach out to others to even try to transform our communities.

Do not doubt our apathy. The very fact that the extremes of each side dominate our politics and our press is testament enough that we simply do not care.

Gandhi said, "No man loses his freedom except through his own weakness." Apathy and weakness are directly related, for our apathy fills us with a listless boredom that lulls us to sleep. How are we to awaken?

Passion

Do you want to see passion? Look at your children. They live at the edge of life. They run at full throttle until they collapse from exhaustion. You will find them, fearless, walking on a dangerous cliff edge or swimming out into the ocean current.

Children take great relish in victory when they succeed. In failure, no amount of consolation can assuage their grief. Fortunately grief has no hold on them. They naturally seem to seek joy and happiness.

In short, children are entirely different creatures than we adults. They have a passion for life we've forgotten. This is why Jesus said, "Unless you become like children you will never enter the Kingdom of Heaven." Children remind us of *the way we were created to be*.

Do you think we are meant to be mired in grief and boredom for years? Are we destined for hate and isolation and despair? No! Every part of my being cries out against that verdict.

We were designed for *more*! That's one of the most common feelings of men. We know we ought to be more than we are. We have a desperate yearning for something better that always seems to be just over the horizon.

Our children *already live in the world we long for:* an immense joy infuses all their days. Of course in this fallen world, we will not easily realize that passion. We catch only glimpses of the joy meant to be a permanent part of our lives.

One means of recapturing joy is to awaken to a life of passion. We understand the meaning of the word when we say, "He has a passion for music." "She is passionate about her vocation." What does that life look like?

There are great people in our culture who have lived passionate lives. Here is a short list: Michael Jordan, Tom Brady, Bill Gates, Mother Theresa, John Paul II, Billy Graham. What do ball players and business tycoons have in common with saints and evangelists? Their passion for their work has been so focused that it drives them to greatness in their chosen field.

What about the rest of us? Many whose names you have never heard have moved others, transforming lives and their world. Yet most of us in this country don't live up to such a high standard.

How do we recapture the passion we had as children? How can we imitate the zeal we see in those who move the world today? How do we create a passionate response to those whose obsession will destroy our nation?

There are no quick and easy answers to these questions, for our normal tendency is to go the easy path, to not confront or stand against the destruction we see around us. But we must awaken. We must not conform to this world but be transformed by the renewing of our minds. (Romans 12.2)

That awakening begins in a purposeful program of reaching out to others in the conviction that *they matter.* The central core of the program I am laying out for our reconciliation is a series of steps that will convince others that they *matter* to us! That they are loved and cherished — even though we may disagree with their philosophy or opinions or lifestyle.

The great challenge is we will not carry through with the steps I outline unless we are lifted out of the shallow grave of apathy we have chosen. Will we stand?

So I sat quietly, agreed politely.
I guess that I forgot I had a choice.
I let you push me past the breaking point.
I stood for nothing, so I fell for everything.
... Get ready 'cause I had enough.
I see it all, I see it now.
I got the eye of the tiger, a fighter
Dancing through the fire
'Cause I am a champion, and you're gonna hear me
ROAR[19]

---

[19] Perry, Katy *"Roar"*

How We Heal

"First of all, then, I urge that supplications, prayers, intercessions and thanksgivings be made for all men, for kings and all who are in high positions, that we may lead a quiet and peaceable life, godly and respectful in every way."
(1 Timothy 2.1,2.)

"Prayer from the heart can achieve what nothing else can in the world."
Mahatma Gandhi

"Love your enemies and pray for those who persecute you." *(Matthew 5.44)*

"Now faith is the assurance of things hoped for, the conviction of things not seen."
(Hebrews 11.1)

Ten: The First Step: Pray

We've heard it in recent years from both sides: "He's not my president." Trump, Obama, Bush, Clinton. We are the kingmakers — and we cannot stand when the other side's ruler wins. What if we prayed for our leaders, no matter their party or belief?

Is there a correlation between praying for our leaders and leading quiet and peaceable lives? Imagine how much more peace we would have if we simply stopped decrying the choice of President. We might find more important worries in our lives. We could then discover common ground with the loyal opposition.

The call to pray for this nation and to heal our divisions is not just for Christians but for all faiths and for those of no faith. Whether you are Buddhist, Muslim, Jewish, Hindi, Bahai or of any other faith or belief, pray! The act of prayer changes who we are and how we think of others.

For my friends who are unbelievers, I know what you're thinking. Like you, I was an atheist for many years. If you've read this far, you will know why I became a believer. I still remember, though, what my reactions were to someone's call to pray. "Absurd! Mysticism. What a waste of time. Prayer doesn't solve anything. Why don't you *do* something about the problem!"

I understand. Yet I beg your indulgence. For us believers, prayer is simply a conversation which happens to be with Jesus (or Yahweh, Buddha or Allah.) I do not ask you to pray. I do ask you to have a conversation with someone radically different than yourself; perhaps with a Catholic like me. You will probably have to work at seeking common ground but you will be amazed at how quickly you find it.

I ask you further to reflect within yourself. Think quietly and deeply, "What can I do to heal the divisions we all have created in this nation?" Each of us must look within ourselves to change who *we* are, not seek to change others.

Remember our goal is to see one another as Thomas Merton saw those around him, "all walking around shining like the sun." We cannot hold hate within our hearts and see others that way. Whether we use prayer or simply contemplate the value of others, that is the first step. Change begins first within us.

We will not find transformation in political solutions, which fuel division. What can you personally change? What local problem might we find to solve together? As President John F. Kennedy said in his Inaugural Address, "Ask not what this country can do for you. Ask what you can do for this country."

Now I address my fellow believers and critique especially my fellow Christians. Some seventy-five percent of our nation still claims to be Christian. Though I do not doubt anyone's faith, I charge we have become lukewarm in our witness, primarily in our prayer life. As I stated above in my chapter on Apathy, we are guilty even above others. We have good news to share and will not step out to do so.

We are not praying for this nation. We are not praying for our neighbors, for the other political party or for our leaders. Instead, we harp and critique and complain like everyone else. How are we to be "salt if our saltness is gone"? How can we witness of we do not display the primary tool of Christian action: prayer?

We would do well to remember that the zealous prayer of the early Christians carried the Church into every corner of the world. Our current churches seem hollow and listless in comparison.

Do we have an example of prayer for our nation and how it might heal our divisions? There is no better example than our first president's prayer.

At the close of the Revolutionary War in 1783, George Washington wrote to the thirteen governors to disband the army and send his troops home. Washington's June 14, 1783 letter to the governors included this prayer for them and for our young nation:

"I now make it my earnest prayer that God would have you, and the State over which you preside, in his holy protection; that he would incline

the hearts of the citizens to cultivate a spirit of subordination and obedience to government, to entertain a brotherly affection and love for one another, for their fellow citizens of the United States at large, and particularly for brethren who have served in the field; and finally that he would most graciously be pleased to dispose us all to do justice, to love mercy, and to demean ourselves with that charity, humility, and pacific temper of mind, which were the characteristics of the Divine Author of our blessed religion, and without an humble imitation of whose example in these things, we can never hope to be a happy nation."

Could you imagine our nation if our leaders all prayed like Washington? It would not be divided, an Alien Nation seeking to tear itself apart. A more caring, more welcoming nation would be stronger and greater than today.

Understand that prayer is not asking God to change our surroundings. The verse I cited above from Paul's letter to Timothy called for early Christians to pray for their leaders *in the times when those leaders were sending Christians to their death by the thousands.* Prayer is not designed to change those around us, but to change us.

Prayer like Washington's is what we need. From the greatest to the most humble, we need to pray in earnestness and zeal. We need prayer to heal this nation: prayer outside of the church; prayer at work, in the marketplace, at school, in the streets and communities and cities and in the home where husbands and wives pray together over their children.

This call for prayer may seem already divisive to some. After all, we have been told that prayer or religion do not belong anywhere outside the home or the walls of the church. That claim ignores the very essence of our prayer life and our witness as Christians, Jews, Muslims, Buddhists, etc.

Anyone who truly follows their faith or any belief knows it does not simply apply to private action or to religious services. Every religion calls its followers to walk out their faith in all aspects of their lives: family, community, work, school and nation.

We try to build a wall of separation between Church and State. We cannot build a wall of separation between Church and Life. Those who ask us to do so ask the impossible of us.

Let's return to Washington's prayer. What can we learn from it? How does each clause contrast to the state of our nation today?

"I now make it my earnest prayer that God would have you ... in his holy protection ..." We have forgotten to ask God for His holy protection. Our enemies such as Iran, Isis, and radical terrorists have not.

On the domestic front, the most radical elements seek to destroy the peace and foment hatred. They rejoice when we take sides and give into polarization and alienation. We are called to pray against this type of hatred.

"... that he would incline the hearts of our citizens to cultivate a spirit of subordination and

obedience to government ..." I find this part of Washington's prayer ironic. Washington had just lead a successful revolt against the government of Great Britain. Now he asked our citizens to cultivate a spirit of subordination. Washington knew both war and peace intimately. He knew the spirit of rebellion and the spirit of subordination and that only the latter could provide a "quiet and peaceable life."

"... to entertain a brotherly affection and love for one another," This nation now seems more divided than at any time since the Civil War. We stand in two vast camps set across a chasm of condemnation and ready for battle over the smallest slight. We have become an Alien Nation. This very brotherly affection and love for one another fueled Thomas Merton's vision and will be the centerpiece of our reconciliation.

"... for their fellow citizens of the United States at large," Yes, even for those in the opposing political camps who sometimes seem so alien. And, for those in California and New York and Mississippi and Texas when sometimes we'd *like* to see them secede from the union.

"Particularly for brethren who have served in the field;" We should pray for and serve our veterans who sacrificed so much that we might savor the rare freedom we have in this nation. In the midst of our partisan bickering we allow those who sacrificed so much to go hungry and homeless.

"... and finally that he would most graciously be pleased to dispose us all to do justice, to love

mercy ..." Washington did well to place these two together. Today we seek justice for others, condemning those who disagree in the most virulent terms. Yet we want mercy for ourselves, proposing that our own sins be ignored. We will only be able to live together in peace when we reverse that formula, giving mercy to others and requiring the strictest justice for ourselves.

For Christians, our God is one of Justice and Mercy combined. The relatives of the nine saints of Mother Emmanuel AME stood before the man who murdered their loved ones and forgave him. Yet they still wanted to see proper justice done.

"... and to demean ourselves with that charity, humility, and pacific temper of mind," Let's break this down.

Charity: Washington calls us to serve one another, to help, and to reach out in love.

Humility: He calls us to Humility, a rare quality in our time of celebrity and instant fame.

Pacific temper of mind: Could we use more of that! Prayer will focus our thoughts to listen for the still, small voice instead of screaming at one another.

"...which were the characteristics of the Divine Author of our blessed religion," Washington's prayer is unapologetically Christian. Who today in government or public life dares to pray like this? If we Christians were as firm and unapologetic about our faith, we would provide those who oppose us with a clearer understanding of our own vision. Yet how often do we Christians express our love for others like

Washington and Thomas Merton did?

"... and without an humble imitation of whose example in these things, we can never hope to be a happy nation." What leader today has the moral authority and strength to defer "in humble imitation" to our Lord? The foundation of Washington's authority lies in a deep and abiding prayer-filled life with Christ.

"... we can never hope to be a happy nation."

Are we a happy nation? Would anyone dare to say we are? Can prayer help? Yes! I have seen prayer transform churches, non-profits, businesses and individuals to bring them alive! It transformed me from atheist to believer.

Prayer was at the heart of the Mother Emmanuel Nine, murdered by someone who could not see the beauty of who they were. Prayer fortified their sons and daughters, brothers and sisters and enabled them to forgive that young man. Their prayer and their action will never be forgotten. It resonates still today because of our ongoing prayers for peace here and throughout this country.

Great things are coming, a great revival for this nation. My friend Senator Tim Scott always speaks with great hope for America, but his hope lies in the strength of his prayer life. His hope is in a vision that does not look back to the times before. Tim knows we do not want to return to a past with its own darkness and division. He looks forward to a nation filled with a passion for life based on our love for God and for our fellow countrymen.

How do we find that love for our nation and our countrymen? We begin with prayer.

"Love your enemies and pray for those who persecute you." That is incredibly difficult. I will tell you we cannot do so without deep prayer. The human side of us wants *them* to change. I understand. I would like nothing better than for all my opponents to see things the way I do. That's not only unrealistic; it's definitely not what Jesus has commanded. I love and pray for my enemies so that I might change how *I see them*; that I might see them as God does: "shining like the sun."

For my unbelieving friends, I hope you have held onto the idea of deep contemplation of the value of others. What you'll find when you do is your thoughts about them resemble what we believers call "prayer." When we see them as more than a bundle of beliefs and actions we condemn, we cannot help but begin to want what is for their good. We might want to then reach out to them and begin to really get to know them.

With a firm hold on that vision of others they — and we — will begin to shine.

We must never lose hope. If we once again become a praying nation, we will find God's blessings poured out abundantly on us. Never lose hope. Pray, for "faith is the assurance of things hoped for, the conviction of things not seen."

Do you not yet see others shining? Look more deeply.

"A sower went out to sow. ...Other seeds fell on good soil and brought forth grain, some a hundredfold, some sixty, some thirty. He who has ears, let him hear." (Matthew 13.3-8)

"I offer you peace. I offer you love. I offer you friendship. I see your beauty. I hear your need. I feel your feelings." Mahatma Gandhi

"...'Lord, when did we see you hungry and feed you, or thirsty and give you drink? And when did we see you a stranger and welcome you, or naked and clothe you? And when did we see you sick or in prison and visit you?' And the King will answer them, 'Truly, I say to you, as you did it to one of the least of these my brethren, you did it to me." (Matthew 25. 37-40)

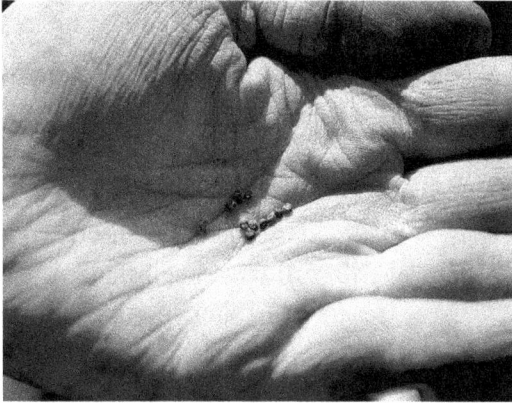

Eleven: The Second Step: Sow

The next step in our healing process is to "Sow." Though the idea seems simple enough it will demand something we all seem to have little of today: patience.

Bishop Mark Lawrence of the Anglican Diocese of South Carolina used the image of the sower in his sermon to the Diocesan Convention this year.

The Anglican Church in South Carolina is in an extended court battle for the rights to historic church properties and over other deeper issues of belief and practice. Bishop Lawrence warned his congregation that this battle is ongoing and the outcome uncertain.

His sermon reminded them that they are not called to fight legal feuds over worldly things, but are called to preach the good news and to make disciples. Thus his message was, "Listen, a sower went out to sow. We are called to sow. Let us follow our calling in this year by spreading the Gospel of Jesus Christ."

I thank Bishop Lawrence because his preaching

struck my heart and showed me this second step. "A sower went out to sow." We Christians are called to share the good news that God loves us. We think it's an easy task until we remember our history.

Christ's call leads us to lives in contrast to the flow of culture. It has always been that way. Culture has never wanted to hear such news. Thus martyrs were made in the early days of the church and are still being killed throughout the world today. Yet we must sow.

The image of the sower is one of gentleness. Back then the act of sowing was not like today's mechanized systems, but was done by hand. The sower walked and cast the seed out in a gentle arc across the field. He did not concern himself with making sure every grain hit the fertile soil. Some fell on the path or on rocky soil or among thorns. His job was to sow.

We are called to share the gospel with gentle deeds and words. We have learned through many costly lessons that, as St. John Paul II said, "We do not wish to impose but to *propose*." Jesus told Pilate "My Kingdom is not of this world." Paul exhorted his church to "pray for those in authority and for the Emperor" in a time when Rome sought to stamp out all vestiges of the young church. Augustine wrote of the "City of Man and the City of God" and how those two should not and cannot be combined. Christianity is not a religion seeking theocracy, nor one calling for revolution or domination of others. It seeks to win hearts through sharing the good news.

My exhortation to every American is the same. "Sow." You want to reach others to convince them to see things as you do. What will work if you want to succeed? We will require gentleness and kindness. Screaming and violence do not work. Political wrangling is useless. Vociferous insisting that "I am right!" has never worked. What are we to do? How do we sow? Let's learn from the teacher who first told us about the Sower.

Again, I write this from my Christian perspective but the principles apply no matter your belief.

In his time, Jesus did not go to Rome to confront Caesar or petition for his people. He did not go up to Jerusalem to debate with the Scribes and the Pharisees about the points of the law. He went out to those in need. He healed the sick and fed the poor. He shared the good news that God loves us.

"The sower went out to sow." We are called to action. Sowing has always meant that we first act as Christians should. Peter tells us, "Maintain good conduct among [unbelievers], so that in case they speak against you as wrongdoers, they may see your good deeds and glorify God on the day of visitation." (1Peter 2.12)

One of the greatest tragedies of the Christian Church today is that our actions do not match our Christian beliefs. We have become conformed to the world rather than being transformed by the Holy Spirit. The divorce rate among Christians varies so slightly from our secular counterparts. This is only one sad statistic that testifies against us. Were we to "sow," through our actions in living as Christ calls us to live, we would transform this nation. Yet we do not.

Sowing calls us to action by reaching out to others. Jesus taught us how we are to sow. "…'Lord, when did we see you hungry and feed you, or thirsty and give you drink? And when did we see you a stranger and welcome you, or naked and clothe you? And when did we see you sick or in prison and visit you?' And the King will answer them, 'Truly, I say to you, as you did it to one of the least of these my brethren, you did it to me." (Matthew 25.35-40)

Within that passage is no call to speak, to exhort or to condemn. We are told to clothe, feed, give drink and to visit the sick and imprisoned. "When you did it to one of the least of these my brethren, you did it to me." In the Gospels we see Jesus time and again reach out to "sinners," to those outcasts of the time about whom no one else cared.

In a later conference entitled "A Work to Do," Bishop Lawrence referenced the remarkable growth of the early church. One reason he points to is that early Christians "provided new norms and new social structures to cope with the serious problems of their day."[20] They did what Jesus had told them to do.

They took care of widows and orphans, fed the poor, visited those in prison and reached out to heal the sick. The structures they built into their lives

---

[20] Lawrence, Bishop Mark . *"A Work to Do"* 9/29/18

created a new culture capable of making life more tolerable in a world torn by strife and war.

We come to the "doing" part of our job. The Letter of James says "But be doers of the word, and not hearers only, deceiving yourselves." (James 1.22) We most effectively reach one another through action. As Saint Francis adds, "At all times preach the Gospel; when necessary use words."

In America we step up to help when disaster strikes or the need arises. We go out and sow. After a hurricane, a mass shooting, a house fire or an accident, people give. We bring food and clothing. We provide shelter or we donate to help do so. Whether Christian, Buddhist, Muslim or non believer, we sow good into peoples lives.

Why don't we make that practice a constant in our lives? It certainly seems our nation is in a continual crisis of division. Let's use that as a starting point to reach out to one another.

We find in working to help others that we begin to care about them. They become more important to us than we could have imagined. They are real to us for the first time. They matter to us. They begin to "shine."

When we work together to answer a pressing need in our own community, we come to understand one another. There is so much need and so much we can do on a local basis. Let's find common ground and fertile soil. "The sower went out to sow."

"Every day they continued to meet together in the temple courts. They broke bread in their homes and ate together with glad and sincere hearts…" (Acts 2.46)

"Let us Break Bread Together (African American Spiritual)

"True love is born of understanding."
Buddha

Twelve: The Third Step: Eat

I had a conversation with a friend.

"We'll find in working to help others that we begin to care about them. They become more important to us than we could have imagined. They are real to us for the first time. They will begin to *shine*."

"How? How is it possible to see beauty in *them*?"

"I know a practical way to discover the beauty and dignity of your enemies."

"Really? I don't buy that. How?"

"Invite them to dinner."

"Oh, come on! *Them*?"

"In your home."

"What? Are you crazy? Those people ... in *my house*? They're _____." (fill in the blank.)

"Yes they might be exactly what you think they are. And, they are so much more you haven't bothered to ask about. So ask. Get to know them. You will be shocked and pleasantly surprised. And you will have made new friends. I guarantee it."

We take the third foundational step in healing our divisions. We must eat. You might think, "Eat? What does that have to do with alienation?" We prayed for the nation. We sowed in working to help others. If we are to reach across the divide, we must break bread together. We must eat.

Our divisions in this nation have lead to a parched and toxic desert landscape where we yield nothing to one another because we refuse to see each other. We cannot harvest hope, understanding and love by sowing despair, division and hate. In this we are all guilty. We judge the other side as "snowflakes" or "bigots"; as "blind" or "stupid." We congratulate ourselves on the virtue of our positions while we condemn and alienate our next door neighbor.

Paul's exhortation to the Galatians speaks to us today. "You, my brothers and sisters, were called to be free. But do not use your freedom to indulge your passions; rather, serve one another humbly in love. For the entire law is fulfilled in keeping this one command: 'Love your neighbor as yourself.' If you bite and devour each other, watch out or you will be destroyed by each other". (Gal. 5.13-15)

We are doing exactly that today. We bite and devour one another and are well on the way to destroying one another.

Instead of dividing we must increase our understanding. We must fertilize the parched soil by watering and feeding the fragile shoots just beginning to grow from those times of crisis that have united us in the past.

But how do we possibly bridge the divisions we ourselves have created? I again return to Thomas Merton's vision, the keystone of this entire book. Merton saw those strangers who passed by him and realized he loved them because they and he were the same: "made in God's image." They were "shining like the sun."

This invitation to break bread together should be easier for us Christians. After all, Jesus did it all the time! He ate with "tax collectors and sinners." Moreover, he explicitly commanded us, "Love your enemies." Yet we too hesitate to reach out to our "enemies." We also say, "How is it possible to ask *those people* into our homes?" The answer lies in Merton's vision which reflected the deeper and truer knowledge Jesus has of us.

Our Lord already knew the "tax collectors and sinners" just as he knows us. Jesus sees the heart and essence of who they were — and who we are — chosen for life, wrought in wonder, deeply loved and meant for royal splendor, we shine like the sun.

We are made in His image. Do we really understand what that means for us — and for every single other person we ever encounter? C.S. Lewis said; "There are no ordinary people. You have never talked to a mere mortal. …it is immortals whom we joke with, work with, marry, snub and exploit…"[21]

We Christians are called today to stand in the midst of the alienation dividing us and to testify

---

[21] Lewis, C.S. "The Weight of Glory"

of God's unifying vision of man. That has always been the Gospel message. We are to reach out to those lost and alone and invite them in.

The blogger Austin Ruse wrote that he had made friends with at least two different blogger "enemies." He concluded in speaking about one blogger, "We disagree profoundly on what both of us see as one of the vitally important issues of our day. But, somewhere along the line, we broke that fourth wall. He is now more than a set of wrong-headed and even harmful opinions as, I suspect, am I. He is a human being. He is my friend."[22]

Ruse discovered this depth of caring even without breaking bread with the man. He simply took that dangerous first step: reach out to your opponent and get to know him. Imagine if you, too, could break the wall separating us. Isn't it worth the try?

How then are we to implement such a program? The way I recommend is to expand on a proposal of Senators Tim Scott and James Lankford. They call it "Solution Sundays" and describe it as follows:

"What if Americans intentionally took action to build relationships and build trust across racial lines by spending intimate time together…? Let us ask you this question…have you ever had dinner in your home with a person of another race? Engaging on the personal level in your own home is an act that could break down walls and build trust across many of our communities. When we start listening to one another,

---

[22] Ruse, Austin, *"Slowly Boiled Friendship?"* Crisis 7/20/18

we gain more respect for our fellow man."[23]

In their book *Unified,* Tim Scott and Trey Gowdy describe how the simple act of dining together overcame decided differences between them and helped to form a lasting bond of friendship. They also found that dining together with opponents even helped to overcome the natural animosity that seems to arise from political opposition in Washington.

The racial divide is simply the most obvious. Let us extend this invitation across all the other divisions: Christian and Atheist; Republican and Democrat; Liberal and Conservative; Pro-Life and Pro-Choice, etc. Include all the other movements and moments out there. Who has the courage to risk dining with those who they think are the "least among us?" Who will break bread…with me?

> "Sometimes it seems to me
> That this world is only where we start.
> For all it's wonder I still believe
> The answer lies deep within our hearts.
> Baby, here I stand unafraid
> To give myself, to be set free.
> In love we find, there is no end.
> We've always been
> We'll always be
> Everlasting."[24]

---

[23] Senators Tim Scott and James Lankford, 7/20/16

[24] McDonald, Michael & Jennings, Waylon "Blink of an Eye" 1993

"As I have loved you, so you must also love one another." (John 13.34)

"It is easy to hate and it is difficult to love. This is how the whole scheme of things works. All good things are difficult to achieve, and bad things are very easy to get." Confucius

"Greater love hath no man than this, that he lay down his life for his friends." (John 15.13)

"Our ability to reach unity in diversity will be the beauty and test of our civilization." Mahatma Gandhi

"I tell you, love your enemies ..." (Matthew 5.44)

"For God so loved the world..." (John 3.16)

Thirteen: The Final Step: Love

Roger winced. He looked at the two angels who had come to visit him. They were talking about a destructive force unmatched by any weapon ever fashioned. And they called it elegant. Despair gripped his heart. "Why don't you simply let us do it? Let us destroy ourselves. Do we deserve to live?"

The angel looked at Roger, the companion who first spoke with him all those years ago. An expression crossed his face which filled Roger with absolute horror. It was one of ruthless judgment, not tempered by mercy. Absolute, complete. The eyes of this being of energy blazed with fire. "My love and I debated this very issue many times. If one considered only what man does, then my answer must be 'No.' Your kind does not deserve to live."

"Then why? Why not let us destroy ourselves?"

The two forms held hands. The light that formed them began to fade and disburse. From within the fading light came a whispered answer. "Love. That was the gift your kind showed us, Roger. It is the reason the answer to your question is tempered. Not that man deserves to live, nor has he since Eden's fall. But that he is loved by God…and that he loves."[25]

*   *   *

We come to the final step of reconciliation in our country. It's the same step we began with long ago. Love is the answer; the only means to solve our problems.

Love. That's easy! We can do that, right? No. Without Christ, true love is impossible. We think we know what love is, but for the most part we hold a very self-centered type of love. Our modern world defines love as an easy emotion, the result of a two hour romantic comedy. Most of us treat love as a bargain, a 50/50 give and take for our own benefit: loving for our own interest, for the feelings love brings, for the support our partner gives, etc.

Contrast our modern shallow idea of love with the Forever Love of Jesus Christ. The love Jesus speaks about is not at all like the love we know today. He tells us "love your enemies and pray for those who persecute you." "Greater love hath no man than this, that he lay down his life for his friends." These are on a completely different plane than our ideas of physical love, or romantic love or even the love and commitment we feel for our spouse.

This again is not the kind of love we could hope to achieve on our own. This total outward focus is so

---

25 Stringer, Joseph "The Chosen" 2015

beyond our human nature that we only experience it when drawn into it or even forced to step outside ourselves to give away an extravagant love.

Anyone who has lived in a committed marriage or had children knows that love is difficult to achieve and maintain. Love is not an emotion but the pure fire of will. You love no matter what. Human beings — including those we love — do terrible things. Those you love may cheat, murder, destroy, harm themselves, abandon you. Yet you still love them.

Love them and face Alzheimers, cancer, alcoholism, addiction or death. Love carries you through it. Love them when they break your heart and crush it beyond your ability to bear. Love them when they tear you down to raw pain and despair. When you have done so, you will have touched the surface of an ocean of love that is the essence of Jesus' love for us.

"Love your enemies." We must delve into a love that is impossible without God's strength and witness. As I said before, just thirty-six hours after the horror of their loss, the brothers, sisters, sons and daughters of the Mother Emmanuel Saints faced the man who had murdered their loved ones. They told him, "I love you and I forgive you."

How is such a statement possible? I don't think I would have had the strength of faith to make it.

What drove their statement? Years of prayer and deep study of God's word. I have spoken with several of the family members. They admit their first response was righteous anger and the desire for retribution. Many in Charleston wanted to lash out — to riot and destroy as had happened in other cities.

Even entering the courtroom, some family members wanted to condemn the murderer. Yet Jesus had spoken to them through His word all their lives: "Love your enemies." "Forgive us our trespasses as we forgive those who trespass against us."

God's Holy Spirit supported them. "Lo, I am with you always…" "I will pray the Father, and he shall give you another Comforter…" The Holy Spirit of God spoke through those family members, his voice reflecting their years of prayer and study.

Another example of this great love is Robert Kennedy's speech on the day Martin Luther King was assassinated. He spoke in the heart of Indianapolis to an African American crowd and told them the devastating news that King was dead. He shared with them in their sorrow, then said, "… you can be filled with bitterness, with hatred, and a desire for revenge. We can move in that direction as a country, in great polarization — black people amongst black, white people amongst white, filled with hatred toward one another."

"Or we can make an effort, as Martin Luther King did, to understand and to comprehend, and to replace that violence, that stain of bloodshed that has spread across our land, with an effort to understand with compassion and love."[26]

The heart of our Christian belief in action is

---

[26] Kennedy, Robert. Indianapolis, Indiana, April 4, 1968

"Love your enemies." It is the most demanding and difficult thing to do. We are not normally wired that way. Instead of love and forgiveness we want retribution and condemnation.

We Christians recognize we cannot hope to find that kind of forgiveness on our own. We need constant prayer and deep study of God's word. Therein are the foundations upon which we will build a bridge of reconciliation and conquer our alienation.

The purest vision of the way we should love sometimes reflects total sacrifice. We lay down our lives for others. Or we display an agonized decision to forgive. More often love comes to life in simple giving of our time and talent to build together with those we don't yet know.

Pray. Love is the motivation for prayer. When you love, you pray for those who persecute you.

Sow. Love is the reason to sow. When you love, you reach out to connect with others.

Eat. Love is the food we eat in our common meal. When you love, you share your life.

Love. When you love, you seek only the good of the other and not your own need.

Do we wish to bridge the chasm that separates us from one another? The rage and violence are driven by some few extremists among us. We decry their excesses but we drink of the poison, learning to hate and judge and destroy with words.

Do we want to understand society's divisions? War, murder, theft, riot, violence, rape, hate, envy, abuse: the ultimate cause for all of these is our failure to love.

Love does not require you to be a Christian (though it is the one belief system that placed Love at the very center of all existence, of man and of his relationship to the world and to others.)

There are many other beliefs and systems that recognize this same truth: we find greatness within us when we reach beyond our self interest to help others, to get to know them and to love them. Love brings its healing power to the world and to us individually.

I had a conversation about this book with a good friend who is not Christian.

I told him, "One spark that drove me to write the book was the Las Vegas shooter. His alienation lead him to his act of violence and murder."

My friend responded, "I don't buy that. I have felt the same absolute alienation from everyone, yet I never wanted to go out and kill a bunch of people."

"I accept your point, but there is an important difference between you and the Vegas shooter."

"What?"

"You love other people. In spite of your feelings of alienation, you reach out to help others. You are one of the most giving people I know. You love people. It shows in your actions."

"And the shooter?"

"I don't think he was capable of love. His focus upon his own pain and despair prevented him from knowing the reality of others. He could not *see* them and therefore could not *love* them. He could not even see his own value to those who loved him."

We focus on ourselves rather than others. We demand our rights and fail in love. What of our responsibilities and commitments to those around us? Do they not deserve for us to reach out to them?

Thomas Merton saw those around him "shining like the sun." His vision arose from deep and abiding prayer. For my friends reading this who do not believe, I ask you this one favor. Like you, I once did not believe. You do not have to come to believe as I have. Simply look at the others around you, especially those you find horrible or repulsive. Imagine they are more than you know of them. They are. Imagine they do "shine like the sun." If you simply hold onto that vision for every person you meet, you'll find it will change who you are.

Pray, Sow, Eat and Love. These are the steps we must take to bridge the divides we have created. I can tell you from painful experience it will be the hardest thing you have ever done. It will require the courage to look outside yourself, to reach out as never before. I can also tell you it will be the most rewarding, the richest and greatest blessing you could hope for.

If we simply follow these four steps, we will find our best selves again. We will rebuild what we have lost as a people. We will build a better and greater nation than we knew before, blessed and filled with love so abundant that we will want to share it everywhere. This is the Gospel, the Good News. "As I have loved you, you must love one another." "For God so loved the world…"

"America is not just a country, it's an idea, and real Americans are getting busy."
Bono

"Where there is love there is life."
Mahatma Gandhi

"The best way to find yourself is to lose yourself in the service of others."
Mahatma Gandhi

"The most important thing in the world is family and love." John Wooden

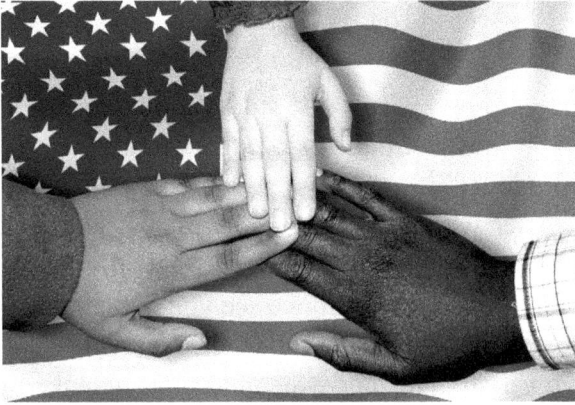

Epilogue: Do Unto Others

"A dream becomes a goal when action is taken toward its achievement." Bo Bennett

"For it is in giving that we receive." Saint Francis of Assisi

"The sole meaning of life is to serve humanity." Leo Tolstoy

"We make a living by what we get; we make a life by what we give." Winston Churchill

"Making money is a happiness; making other people happy is a super-happiness." Muhammad Yunus

"Giving back is as good for you as it is for those you are helping, because giving gives you purpose. When you have a purpose-driven life, you're a happier person." Goldie Hawn

*   *   *

We have so much to do. What keeps us from simply starting? We are all so busy just trying to live or make ends meet or buy that new car or get the kids into the best schools or .... "Busy is an excuse. ... If you're "too busy" for life and people all the time, then you may not be using your 24 hours in the best way possible."[27]

After we have begun these four steps together, we have work to do. Again, Jesus actually describes love this way: "When did we see you hungry and feed you, or thirsty and give you drink? And when did we see you a stranger and welcome you, or naked and clothe you? And when did we see you sick or in prison and visit you? (Matthew 5. 38-40)

The first key in Doing is to *not* ask someone else to make a change. The resolution to our problems is not in Washington, DC or our state capitals. It lies in our hearts. If we love and reach out to help others, we will find our own solutions.

Is there a community you can help rebuild? There are still people in the Houston area and Puerto Rico who are homeless a year after surviving devastating hurricanes. Reach out. Work to help them rebuild and love them.

---

[27] thoughtsrealigned.com 9/9/16

Are there poor and hungry people in your city or town you can help feed? I guarantee they live less than ten miles from you. Don't just give money. Go to the local shelter or soup kitchen. Get to know them. Feed them and love them.

Are people in prison or captives to their own isolation who simply need you there? Can you volunteer at local hospitals, shelters or prisons? They live in isolation. Visit them and love them.

Americans are a giving people. Wherever disaster strikes throughout the world, or in our back yard, we help. But we must help more. We Christians are as guilty as non believers, if not more so. We have been called to give. Our normal standard is to tithe, to give ten percent of our earnings to charity. Yet a very small percentage of us come anywhere close. If we Christians alone would all give ten percent, our social needs would be met to such an extent we could all but eliminate government welfare programs.

Recently, entrepreneur and business coach Rick Jones spoke to our Downtown Businessmen's Luncheon at St. Phillip's Church in Charleston. In his book, *The Business Tithe,* he stated that there are roughly 26 million small businesses in America and of those at least 50 percent are owned by Christian business people. He challenged us. "Small business owners create value for customers, jobs for associates, and give major contributions to the communities they serve. What if the privately held companies owned by Christians tithed 10 percent of their profits and plowed those monies back into rebuilding the communities they live in? We would transform America overnight."[28]

The greatest long term problem we must solve is the alienation of our own children. Here we can make a difference without spending a dime. We need only give love and attention to those closest to us.

Dr. Victoria Prooday, a registered occupational therapist and psychotherapist states, "There is a silent tragedy developing right now in our homes, and it concerns our most precious jewels, our children."

She cites frightening data of this crisis in America. "[I]n the past 15 years, researchers have been releasing alarming statistics on a sharp and steady increase in kids' mental illness, which is now reaching epidemic proportions:

1 in 5 children has mental health problems
43% increase in ADHD
37% increase in teen depression
100% increase in suicide rate in kids from 10 to 14 years old."[29]

Dr. Prooday focuses the responsibility squarely on parents, who fail to provide kids their basic needs of love, attention, guidance and stability. Her

---

[28] Jones, Rick, "The Business Tithe" www.fishbaitbiz.com

[29] Prooday, Dr. Victoria "The Silent Tragedy Affecting Today's Children" www.faithit.com

solutions all involve basic common sense ideas which only require us to give our children what they truly need: our love.

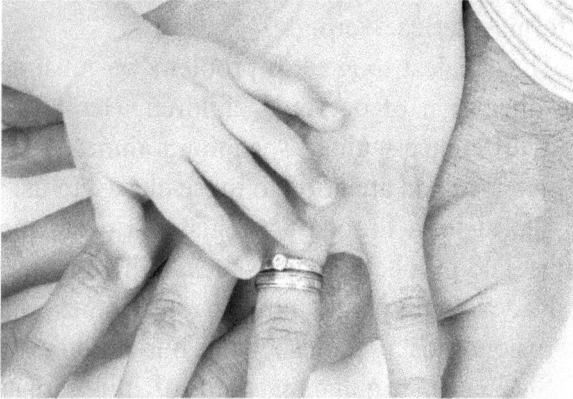

I finish with this example ... and it is here we must begin. If we are to maintain this nation's strength, peace and unity we must start in our homes.

We may and we must begin the job of reconciliation in the steps I have outlined. We need to do so as soon as possible. If we do much of the work outlined above, striving together to transform our communities and cities, we will rebuild our American dream.

But these solutions are focused on short-term answers to physical and social crises. The greater and more long-term crisis lies in our apathy towards providing the nurture and guidance needed for our children. Too long we have neglected them to pursue our own selfish purposes. We have pushed aside the responsibility to others.

The early Christian church set a completely

different example. They saved the unwanted babies who were cast aside by Roman citizens on trash heaps. They adopted them into the family, raising them as their own. They taught them truth and value, giving and honor. They gave them life, and that as abundantly as they could. This can be the greatest gift the early Christian church could possibly bequeath our modern age: love your children.

We must take upon ourselves the responsibility we have abandoned in the last generations. We must rebuild family and home, parents and children as one. Our children need us more now than they ever have. Look at them. They run and play, question and seek, and they discover the wonder of a world of blessing in the love of their parents. Let your children remind you of the joy that is within you. See them as God sees them. They walk around "shining like the sun."

Endnotes

I have focused this book on our reconciliation. We must find the way to live together and love one another in spite of our differences. Within that call are two truths.

First, the call for reconciliation does *not* ignore the reality of evil or sin; of wrong and destructive acts. We must face evil and stand against it. But in doing so, we are required to clearly define its nature and its roots.

Again, I return to the relatives of the Mother Emmanuel Saints. Their forgiveness of the murderer still recognized the evil of the act. They did not excuse his evil actions or ask that justice not be done.

This is the true nature of love. It wants what is best for the other person. Often, that "best" is to help them — with love — to see the error of their ways. We must do so with great care to first clearly define our own prejudices and blindness, our own sinfulness, before seeking to correct the other person. Nonetheless, those of us who are in error need help to correct our ways and to live as God has called us.

Second, the steps to reconciliation of Pray, Sow, Eat and Love cannot happen unless we value something greater than ourselves. We must break out from our own ego and selfishness.

Reconciliation, peace, justice and progress are not possible without an acceptance of an objective existence outside ourselves, an authority to which we owe allegiance (whatever or whomever that may be) other than our own minds.

Reality exists outside of our minds. Truth is the ability to recognize that reality. Reason is the means we use to ascertain truth. Unless we accept these premises there is no way for us to live in communion. We will inevitably resort to political or actual force.

Once we accept the reality of our nature and understand our own faults along with others, we might begin to build the nation anew. There's a great deal of work to do. As Bo Bennett said, "A dream becomes a goal when action is taken toward its achievement." Let's go out and work together.

The following is only a partial list of charities who will welcome your help. There are a thousand more out there. Choose and get involved.

Samaritan's Purse
South Carolina Christian Chamber
Lucis Via
Food for the Poor
Catholic Charities
National Christian Foundation
Ronald McDonald House
Water Missions
Habitat for Humanity
The Salvation Army

Chosen for life, wrought in wonder, deeply loved and meant for royal splendor, you shine like the sun.

ABOUT THE AUTHOR

Joseph Stringer writes and speaks on Christian issues in the current culture. His prayer is that all who read his works might see through them to the One who has chosen us for life.

If you enjoyed *Alien Nation* or have thoughts to share, contact him at his website below.

Stringer's previous works include: *The Ten Commandments for Business,* two novels, a children's illustrated book, music and poetry. His works have been published in various venues in the Charleston, SC area and are available on Amazon.

The U-Pick Farm, published in early 2014, is a delight for children from ages 2 to 12. Read it to them and they'll insist you take them picking.

The novels are set in America in the near future. Stringer is not sure if these books, first envisioned in the 1980s, are fantasy or prophesy. In *The Gem Testament*, Christians have been pushed out of any public setting — something that is coming true today. *The Chosen* finds them hunted throughout America.

Watch for upcoming releases in 2019:

The Ten Commandments for Life: A reflection on how the Ten Commandments direct us to lives filled with grace and love.

Call Me Jonah: Like Jonah, Joseph Stringer ran from God's calling. America, too, has run far from God's clear call for her to be a witness of Christ's saving grace for the world.

Contact the author at: **www.chosen4life.org**
May God the Father, Son and Holy Spirit, bless us and remain with us all the days of our lives.